The Superb Number 7
A Birthday Number Book

by Karin Snelson

Illustrated by Peter Georgeson

**Andrews McMeel
Publishing**

Kansas City

www.andrewsmcmeel.com

The Superb Number 7 is produced by becker&mayer!, Ltd.

ISBN: 0-8362-3220-8
Library of Congress Catalog Card Number: 97-70379

Edited by Alison Herschberg
Illustrated by Peter Georgeson
Book design by Simon Sung
Cover design by Heidi Baughman
Cover illustration by Cary Pillo
Special thanks to Kitty Higgins for her *superb* help on
this book.

ATTENTION: SCHOOLS AND BUSINESSES
Andrews McMeel books are available at quantity discounts
with bulk purchase for educational, business, or sales
promotional use. For information, please write to: Special
Sales Department, Andrews McMeel Publishing, 4520 Main
Street, Kansas City, Missouri 64111.

Congratulations!
Happy birthday!
You are SEVEN
years old! You should
feel lucky, because
SEVEN is a *superb*
number. And this
book will show you why.
Here we go!

ave you ever sung "Old MacDonald Had a Farm"? Here is what "Old MacDonald" looks like written in musical notes. There are seven notes in the musical scale. The seven notes, or *tones*, have the same names as the first seven letters of the alphabet—A, B, C, D, E, F, and G. You mix up the notes to make new music the same way you mix up letters to make new words.

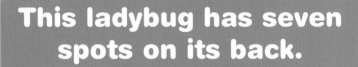

Did you know that there is a kind of ladybug called the seven-spotted ladybug? Ladybugs are friendly looking beetles with round, brightly colored, polka-dotted backs. A ladybug is not, however, just another pretty beetle.

For one thing, ladybugs can eat an amazing number of bugs every day. Their favorite food is a tiny green plant-munching bug called an *aphid* (AY-fid).

Bean farmers and rose gardeners don't like aphids, because aphids eat their prized beans and roses. So they love ladybugs!

The bright-colored, spotted shell of the ladybug is actually a pair of wings. Ladybugs have another pair of wings underneath their shells.

Smells can be grouped into seven categories.

You can smell thousands of different things—toothpaste, burned toast, and skunks, for example.

How does your sense of smell work? Your nose has nerve cells inside of it. Pretend you smell cookies baking in the oven. Tiny bits

Ether   **Musky**   **Floral**   **Pungent**

of cookie are actually floating through the air and into your nose. These bits are so small you can't see them. They are called *molecules* (MOL-eh-kewls). When the cookie molecules reach the nerve cells inside your nose, messages are sent to your brain. Your brain might tell you, "Yum ... cookies!"

Over the years, many scientists have tried to put different smells into groups, or *categories*. A man named Dr. John Amoore divided smells into seven categories.

Here are Dr. Amoore's seven groups of smells: Ether, Musky, Floral, Pungent, Putrid, Camphor, and Peppermint.

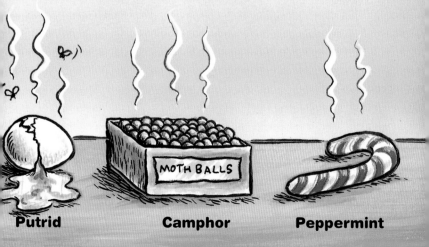

Putrid   **Camphor**   **Peppermint**

Seven is a lucky number.

The number seven has been considered a lucky number for centuries. Perhaps, it's because when you're seven, you go to school and meet new friends, and learn wonderful new things about the world and the people in it. Sometimes, when you're seven years old, you get to ride your bike around the block with your best friend, or go to a movie on Saturday afternoon. Seven is a superb number to be, and you are it! Now, *that's* lucky!

There are seven colors in a rainbow.

The next time you look at a rainbow, count how many colors you can see. Chances are you'll see red, orange, yellow, green, blue, indigo, and violet, in that order. These are the seven colors of

the spectrum. Rainbows appear when white light from the sun enters water droplets in rain, spray, or fog. For you to see a rainbow, the sun must be behind you and the mist must be in front of you. Look for a rainbow the next time it rains!

INDIGO!

The light is reflected through the raindrop.

Sir Isaac Newton (1642–1727) named *indigo,* a purplish color, as the seventh color of the rainbow—a color in between blue and violet. You can remember the colors in a rainbow by saying this name:

Roy G. Biv

R stands for red,
O stands for orange,
Y stands for yellow,
G stands for green,
B stands for blue,
I stands for indigo,
V stands for violet.

There are seven continents on Earth.

Which continent do you live on?

SOUTH AMERICA 2

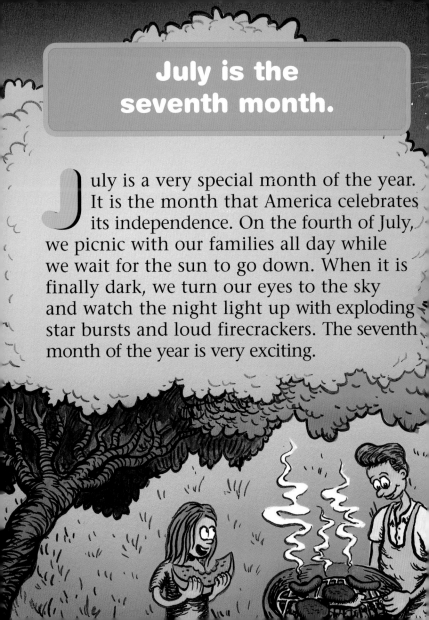

July is the seventh month.

July is a very special month of the year. It is the month that America celebrates its independence. On the fourth of July, we picnic with our families all day while we wait for the sun to go down. When it is finally dark, we turn our eyes to the sky and watch the night light up with exploding star bursts and loud firecrackers. The seventh month of the year is very exciting.

URANUS!

Uranus is a giant ball of gas with rings around it. The planet is far away from the Sun, and very cold. In fact, the top layer of Uranus is made

One of the weirdest things about the planet Uranus is that it looks as if it's tipped over on one side. Some think the planet might have been hit by a huge meteor millions of years ago.

up of frozen gas. Underneath that is a thick layer of water and poison liquids. The center of Uranus is metal.

A giraffe has seven vertebrae in its neck.

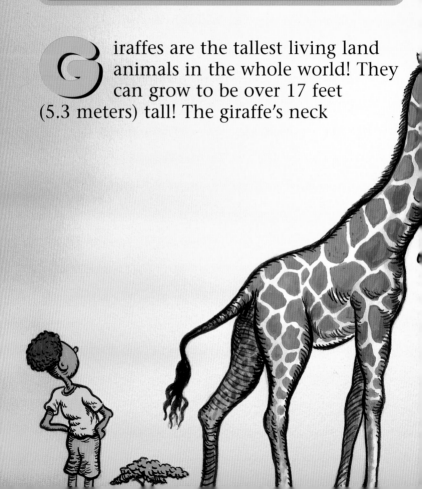

Giraffes are the tallest living land animals in the whole world! They can grow to be over 17 feet (5.3 meters) tall! The giraffe's neck alone is 6 feet (2 meters) long—perfect for reaching the best leaves on the highest trees. On top of that, these towering creatures can see for miles. With such a view, giraffes can spot any hungry lions who might be coming their way.

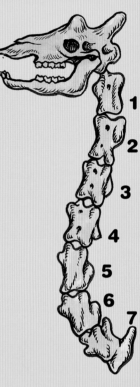

1
2
3
4
5
6
7

Most mammals (even you!) have seven vertebrae in their necks. But no creature has vertebrae as big as a giraffe's.

The Big Dipper has seven stars.

When you look at the night sky and see the Big Dipper, you are actually seeing seven stars. If you drew an imaginary line along them, like connect-a-dot, you'd see a dipper—like a ladle in a bucket of water. Some summer night when you are sleeping outside under the stars, look in the sky for the Big Dipper and imagine taking a dip with that Big Dipper into the Milky Way.

Sail the Seven Seas.

Ancient sailors referred to all the oceans of the earth as the "Seven Seas." They knew that by sailing their boats they could travel to all the mysterious ports of the world. Some of the bodies of water are called *seas* and some are called *oceans,* but no matter what they are called, the Seven Seas are great places for boats to float.

There are seven days in a week.

There are seven days in a week: Monday, Tuesday, Wednesday, Thursday, Friday, Saturday, and Sunday. Did you know that MONday

was named for the Moon, SUNday was named for the Sun, and SATURday was named for Saturn? The other days of the week were named for four "Norse" gods who were popular 1500 years ago in northern Europe. In English, these Norse gods' names were Tiw, Woden, Thor, and Frige. That's why Tiw's Day was Tuesday, Woden's Day was Wednesday, Thor's Day was Thursday, and Frige's Day was Friday.

Seven funny letters.

f I told you that there were seven letters that could make you laugh every time you saw them, what do you think they would be?

If I told you that you watch something with seven letters almost every Saturday morning, what do you think it would be?

If I told you that some of your favorite movies were made up of these seven letters, what kind of movie would you be watching?

"A CARTOON!"

Now you are seven years old!

If you traveled to different parts of the world today, people might say "Happy birthday!" to you, and ask you how old you are. Here's how people might say this in Spanish, French, and German, and how you would answer.

Happy birthday! How old are you?
I am seven years old.

¡Feliz cumpleaños! ¿Cuántos años tienes?
Tengo siete años.

Bonne anniversaire! Quel âge as-tu?
J'ai sept ans.

Glücklicher Geburtstag! Wie alt bist du?
Ich bin sieben Jahre alt.

Why was six afraid of seven?
Because seven ate nine!